Why Are Guns Lethal?

What You Need to Know About What Guns Are And How They Work

by

I0436751

Michael R. Weisser

in collaboration with

William A. Weisser

Published by:

TeeTee Press
Ware MA 01082

Cover design by Damonza

ISBN: 1536814008
ISBN-13: 978-1536814002

10 9 8 7 6 5 4 3 2 1

First Edition

CONTENTS

1. WHAT IS A GUN?

There are many guns out there: water guns, cap guns, nail guns, toy guns. This little book is designed to help you understand one type of gun, which we usually refer to as a firearm. For the purposes of this book, a firearm is any device that can discharge a solid shot or bullet by dint of the energy created by the ignition of a propellant that is located within the same container as the bullet itself. When this container is filled with powder and a bullet, it is called a "cartridge" or a "round."

2. WHAT IS AMMUNITION?

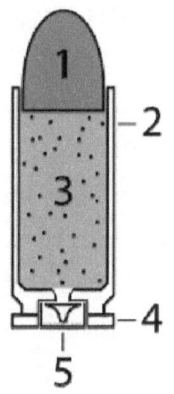

1 – Bullet   2 – Case (or container)   3 – Propellant (gun powder)

4 – Rim   5 – Primer

Now here's how it works. When the outside of the primer (#5) is struck by a sharp piece of metal that we call a "firing pin," the inside of the primer, containing chemical explosives, ignites the powder (#3) whose ignition creates a gas which, as it expands, pushes the bullet (#1) down the barrel. The case (#2) holds the bullet and the propellant in one solid container and the rim (#4) seats the ammunition in the gun. Rimfire cartridges (the ammunition pictured above is a centerfire cartridge) contain the primer chemicals within the back rim of the case.

3. HOW DO WE DIFFERENTIATE DIFFERENT TYPES OF AMMUNITION?

We differentiate different types of ammunition by "caliber," which is usually but not always a measurement of the diameter of the bullet expressed either in inches or millimeters. So, what is commonly referred to as "22-caliber" is a bullet with a width at its widest point of twenty-two one-hundredths (22/100) of an inch. A 9mm round, on the other hand, is 9 millimeters in diameter. But what we call a "38-caliber" bullet isn't 38/100ths of an inch; in fact the actual diameter is .357 inches. On the other hand, what is usually referred to as a "380 round" is the same diameter as a 9mm but is shorter, and in Europe is called a "380 kurz," which is German for "short."

Confused? Good. Here's the bottom line. The easiest way to know what you are talking about is to assume that the first digit is roughly the divider of an inch, no matter what follows. So, a 30-caliber is roughly 30% of an inch wide, a 40-caliber is roughly 40% of an inch wide, and so forth. A 45-caliber bullet or cartridge is therefore almost half an inch wide. Leave it at that.

4. WHAT MAKES DIFFERENT TYPES OF AMMUNITION MORE POWERFUL (AND MORE LETHAL) THAN OTHER TYPES OF AMMUNITION?

The lethality of ammunition is based on the amount of damage caused when the bullet strikes human tissue. The greater the force of the collision between bullet and tissue, the greater amount of damage and the consequent difficulty in repairing the damage. The force of the collision is based on the size of the bullet and the speed at which it is moving when it strikes human tissue.

Bullet speeds are measured from the point at which the bullet exits from the barrel. As the bullet travels away from the barrel it slows down. But since most collisions of bullets and human tissue occur at less than 20 feet, we can use the muzzle speed of bullets as a good guide to determine the lethality of every gun.

Here are some average bullet speeds for standard handgun ammunition that can usually be found in every gun shop or sporting goods store:

.380	900 fps (feet per second)
9mm	1,100 fps
40 S&W	925 fps
45 auto	800 fps

Notice that the bullets with a wider diameter (40 S&W and 45 auto) travel more slowly than the 380 or the 9mm rounds. But they are also considerably heavier; the 45 auto round, for example, is almost twice as heavy as a 9mm round. And remember that the bullet's lethality is a combination of speed and weight, so while the 45 (usually called the 45 ACP) travels 30% more slowly than a 9mm round, it weighs nearly 50% more. Which makes the impact of the 45 ACP bullet greater than the impact of the 9mm.

Now let's look briefly at rifle ammunition. Until the advent of the AR-15, military guns were traditionally designed to take a 30-caliber round, roughly .308 inches in diameter. The 30-caliber round became standard military issue for every U.S. military rifle from 1906 until the AR replaced the M-14 in

1969. Why was the 30-caliber shell adopted? Because it retained its accuracy out to beyond 300 yards, which was required for trench warfare until we started traipsing around in the jungle during Viet Nam.

The 30-caliber military round exits a rifle barrel at roughly 2,800 fps, and hits at the point of impact with seven times more force than a 45 ACP. The AR-15, which fires a 22-caliber bullet, has a velocity that is 15% faster than a 30-caliber round, and hits with four times the force of a 45 ACP. But while the AR doesn't have the impact of an older-style military weapon that fires a 30-caliber shell, it can also fire many more rounds than most (not all) 30-caliber rifles without requiring the shooter to reload.

5. How Do Guns Work?

Every gun is designed so that the back (or the rim) of the cartridge faces the firing pin and the front of the cartridge faces the barrel. The space where the bullet sits before it is fired is called the "breech." What differentiates different types of guns is the mechanism that is used to place each cartridge in that position, but something must be done mechanically to push the firing pin into the primer, and this is usually done by using the trigger to release the hammer which falls on the firing pin and then the gun goes off. Here's a simple diagram:

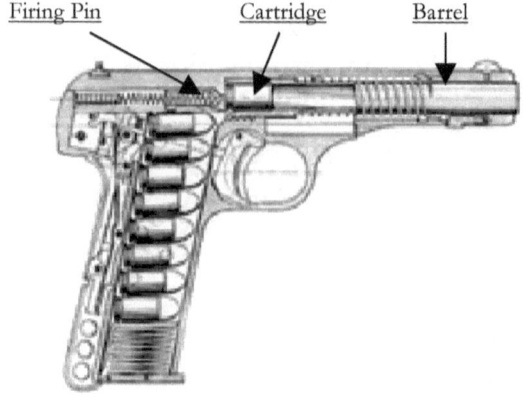

Firing Pin   Cartridge   Barrel

The trigger is usually connected to the hammer with a spring (or multiple springs) called the gun's "action." When the trigger is first pulled, it cocks the hammer and creates a lot of tension in the connecting action so that when the trigger is pulled a little further, the spring is released and lands on the firing pin with great force, thus ensuring that the pin will push all the way into the primer and set off the explosion that ignites the powder.

The cocking and releasing of the hammer is referred to as "double action." In some guns, the shooter has to manually cock the hammer and the trigger is only used to release the hammer so that it can fall on the firing pin. This type of action is called "single action." When the hammer is cocked either with the trigger or manually, it winds around a pin located between the hammer and the trigger called the "sear." After the gun is fired, the sear resets and will not allow the hammer to fall on the firing pin again until the hammer has been cocked again either manually or by using the trigger. By preventing the hammer from falling on the firing pin unless it is cocked, the sear creates what is called 'semi-automatic' mode; i.e., the trigger must be pulled every time it is fired. If the semi-automatic sear is replaced by an automatic sear, it does not re-set into the locked position after every shot, but allows the hammer to keep falling on the firing pin as long as there is ammunition in the gun. *Now you know the difference between a semi-auto and a full-auto gun.*

6. WHAT'S THE DIFFERENCE BETWEEN A HANDGUN AND A LONG GUN?

Generally speaking, a long gun is defined as any firearm with a barrel length of 16 inches or more. Hence, handguns are defined as firearms with barrel lengths of less than 16 inches. Are there exceptions to this rule? There are exceptions to just about every gun rule. But this rule usually holds true, and if you think of long guns as firearms with barrels that are usually at least twice as long as the barrels of handguns, you're on solid ground.

7. TYPES OF LONG GUNS (1): SHOTGUNS

Shotguns fire ammunition that is a group of small, metal pellets rather than one solid bullet. The pellets scatter when a shotgun shell is fired and the pellets exit from the barrel. Otherwise, shotgun ammunition functions in the same way as any other kind of ammunition, and shotguns, like other guns, are designed so that the primer of the shotgun shell faces the firing pin and the pellets face the barrel.

Shotgun ammunition, like handgun and rifle ammunition, is designated by the diameter of the shell. But instead of calibers, the designation is stated in "gauges." There are four standard shotgun gauges and therefore four different shotgun calibers: 12 gauge, 16 gauge, 20 gauge, and 410 gauge. With the exception of the 410, which is actually a caliber, the gauge number refers to the number of lead balls that add up to one pound, so a 12-gauge refers to the diameter of a lead ball that is $1/12^{th}$ of a pound, a 16-gauge would be $1/16^{th}$ of a pound and so forth.

What this means is that a 12-gauge gun has a wider barrel than a 16-gauge gun, which in turn has a wider barrel than a 20-gauge gun. Consequently, a 12-

gauge shell holds more shot than a 16 gauge, and so forth. When the shot exits the barrel, the pattern of how the shot hits the target is determined by the distance from the barrel to the target and the "choke" of the barrel, which is a metal sleeve inserted in the end of the barrel to make the diameter either wider or more narrow.

The pattern of how the shot shell hits the target is also determined by the size of the pellets. Generally speaking, smaller pellets are used for sporting and bird shooting because the pattern is wider since the pellets weigh less and therefore disperse more quickly. On the other hand, shotguns that are used for self-defense (or self-offense) tend to be loaded with heavier, denser shot, usually referred to as 00 Buck ("double ought buck") or 000 Buck ("triple ought buck"), and such shot tends to hit and penetrate with devastating effect due to weight and speed.

The other factor that determines shotgun lethality is the length of the shot shell itself. Shells come in lengths from 2 ¾ inches to 3 ½ inches, the latter usually referred to as "magnum" rounds. A 20-gauge shotgun with a 2 ¾-inch shell is much less lethal than a 12-gauge gun loaded with 00 Buck, the latter gun delivering 18-24 individual pellets at speeds in excess of most handgun loads.

Self-defense or tactical shotguns load either by manually pulling the ammunition from a lower tube into the barrel (while at the same time ejecting the spent case), or by the gun's action pulling the ammunition from a lower tube into the barrel because of the manner in which the gas escapes when the gun is fired.

Here's a semi-auto tactical shotgun:

And here's a pump tactical shotgun:

<u>Fore End Slide</u>

Notice that both guns have what are referred to as "tactical" rails above the trigger so that scopes, lasers and other aiming devices can be easily mounted. Notice that the pump gun has a space between the fore end slide and the receiver so that it can be manually moved back and forth to load the next shell.

Finally, here is a picture of a sporting shotgun:

Break-open Lever

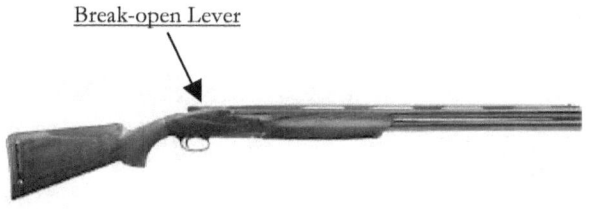

Notice that this gun also has two tubes, but in fact they are both barrels. In order to reload this gun, a lever that sits behind and above the trigger is pulled, the gun breaks open between the receiver and the back of the barrels, the empty shells are ejected and the shooter must reload the gun manually by inserting two new shells into the back of the barrels and snapping the gun shut. Such shotguns are designed for sporting use, either hunting or trap and skeet shooting at a range.

8. TYPES OF LONG GUNS (2): RIFLES

(LEVER ACTION)

Like shotguns, rifles are usually described by the manner in which the ammunition is placed within the gun's breech so that pulling the trigger will result in the gun going off. The oldest design still in service is known as the lever-action rifle, which uses the pulling of a lever behind the trigger to move a shell from the loading tube up into the barrel of the gun:

Lever-action rifles come in many different calibers, both rim-fire and center fire calibers, and are popular for hunting small and medium-size game. These guns also tend to have shorter barrels than bolt-action hunting rifles, they are easy to carry and maneuver if the hunter is walking through woods, and the most popular caliber over the years is called the 30-30 caliber, which first appeared in 1895. Its popularity is due to its extreme accuracy, relatively light recoil and relative slowness (compared to a military 30-06) which allows it to stay on course if it is shot through heavy brush at standing or moving game. Is a gun like this extremely lethal? It has probably killed more white-tail deer than all other hunting calibers combined; it can fire rapidly but once the load is exhausted the time involved in reloading the gun generally rules it out as a tactical weapon of choice. It also cannot be easily rigged with sights or other aiming devices.

(BOLT ACTION)

Bolt-action rifles use a metal tube that contains the sear, the firing pin and the ejector to both move a shell into the firing position within the gun as well as to eject a spent shell if a round has previously been fired. This requires the shooter to manually maneuver the bolt over the source of the ammunition, which is usually housed in a metal holder, known as a magazine, that fits inside the gun between the trigger and the barrel.

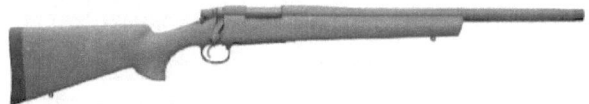

The good news about bolt-action rifles is they tend to be very accurate but they also require time between each shot. But they don't require that much time. A well-trained marksman can get off three accurate shots from a bolt-action rifle in six seconds or less. But manually moving the bolt in and out of a bolt-action breech requires the shooter to re-set the point of aim after every shot. Also, the design of a bolt-action rifle usually limits the ammunition capacity to 6 shots or less. Thus, the lethality of this type of weapon vis-à-vis human targets is important only for long-distance, sniper use.

(Semi-Auto Action)

The advantage of a semi-automatic rifle is that it automates the manual action of a bolt-action gun and requires the shooter only to pull the trigger in order for the gun to fire and reload. Like a semi-automatic handgun, the semi-automatic rifle also contains a sear which prevents the gun from firing more than one shot with each trigger pull, unless the semi-auto sear is replaced by a full-auto sear part.

Semi-automatic rifles come in two basic designs. The older, more traditional design is basically a hunting rifle which has a limited magazine capacity and differs only from the bolt-action hunting rifle insofar as the process of ejecting a spent shell and loading a fresh round is accomplished by the firing of the gun itself, rather than by any manual operation on the part of the person shooting the gun.

Like the bolt-action rifle, this gun can be fitted with a scope but the optics have to be attached by first drilling holes in the top of the receiver and then attaching a set of rings to the receiver which then holds the scope. Most semi-automatic hunting rifles use ammunition in a detachable magazine that can easily be removed and replaced after the last shot, but such magazines only hold 5-6 rounds, depending on the caliber of the gun.

There are also many semi-automatic, mostly surplus military rifles floating around, such as the SKS gun that was evidently used by the shooter in Dallas on July 7, 2016. These guns tend to be 30-caliber weapons. They are fairly accurate but usually require reloading after 10 rounds are fired, and often require top-mounted (hence slower) reloading because the magazine is connected to the stock.

(MODERN ASSAULT RIFLE)

And here is what the gun industry wants you to believe is a "modern sporting rifle," and you can see how similar it is to the real sporting rifle pictured just above. What makes this gun, the AR, different from all modern sporting rifles, is that it is designed specifically to be used in "tactical" situations, which is a polite way of saying that it is used by men to kill other men (and women, and kids). The adjustable stock gives it flexibility and reduces the weight of the gun; the rails make it easy to add optics, lasers, lights and other tactical accoutrements; the pistol grip helps stabilize the weapon and makes it easier and more accurate to deliver 60 rounds in less than one minute; the flash suppressor minimizes muzzle flash when the gun is operated at night.

Why is this gun an assault weapon? Because in 1994 the Federal Government defined an assault weapon as any rifle with a detachable magazine whose design also included two of the five components identified in the picture above. But the *real* reason it is an assault weapon is that it is designed to do one thing and one thing only, and that is to assault human beings and cause great harm. And if you find yourself in an argument with someone who wants to deny the intent of this gun, don't be misled into thinking that perhaps you are wrong and they are correct. They aren't correct. I will deal with that issue at the end of this book.

9. TYPES OF HANDGUNS (1): REVOLVERS

Revolvers move ammunition into the firing position by the rotation of a cylinder which holds five, six, seven or ten rounds, depending on the caliber of the gun. The rotation of the cylinder is accomplished by pulling the trigger which simultaneously cocks the hammer and rotates the cylinder so that the firing pin, when pushed forward by the dropping of the hammer, will ignite a fresh round.

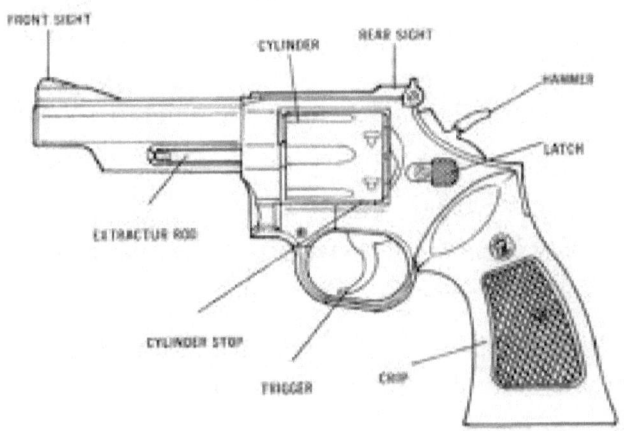

When the cylinder is emptied, the latch is pushed forward (sometimes pulled backward depending on the gun), the cylinder and ejector rod swing away from the frame, and then the ejector rod is pushed forward, thus emptying the spent shells which can then be replaced manually with fresh rounds. The good news about revolvers is that with a 2-inch barrel they are quite small and light; the bad news is that the cylinder usually only holds 5 or 6 rounds, and reloading takes some time. So the guns are very lethal because the penetration and damage caused by modern, magnum-style handgun ammunition is very severe, but the lethality is limited by the low capacity of the guns.

10. TYPES OF HANDGUNS (2): SEMI-AUTOMATIC PISTOLS

Semi-automatic pistols combine the concealability of revolvers with the ability to deliver maximum amounts of firepower both because of high-capacity magazines (as many as 18 rounds or more) as well as the fact that an empty magazine can be replaced by another, fully-loaded magazine in two seconds or less. In effect, semi-automatic pistols have the same degree of lethality as AR rifles, the only difference being that handgun ammunition is not as lethal as rifle rounds, but at a close distance this distinction usually doesn't mean very much.

The pistol above holds 18 rounds. It can also take an extended magazine that holds 30 rounds but makes the gun less concealable. This issue can be readily solved by placing an 18-round magazine in the gun and keeping a 30-round magazine in a pocket; fire the 18 rounds in 15 seconds, drop the empty magazine and replace with the 30-shot mag. Resume firing and shoot a total of nearly 50 rounds in one minute or less.

11. A NOTE ON "HI-CAP" GUN MAGAZINES

Gun magazines, or what are also called ammunition-feeding devices, are used to hold ammunition until it is needed to be placed in position where it can be fired. Most magazines are metal boxes that fit into the gun either in the grip or underneath the gun in front of the trigger. The ammunition can also be fed from a tube that sits underneath the barrel.

In some rifles, the magazine is an integral part of the gun itself and it not detachable from the gun. These guns must be reloaded either by pushing individual rounds down into the magazine or by using a thin piece of metal which holds a number of rounds together and lets the shooter reload a group of rounds at one time.

Magazine capacity was never standardized by gun makers, and ranges from 3-4 rounds for hunting rifles to 30 rounds or more for military-style assault rifles. Pistol magazines are generally 7-18 rounds, depending on the size of the gun and the ammunition, but after-market extended magazines can be acquired that double the capacity of the weapon.

In 1994, as part of the assault weapons ban, the Federal Government mandated that no new long gun or handgun could be sent to market with a magazine whose capacity was in excess of 10 rounds (law enforcement weapons were exempt from this requirement). Nobody knows why 10 rounds was determined to be the cut-off number that defined a high-capacity or "hi-cap" magazine. One story is that it was done for the convenience of Bill Ruger, whose 22-caliber sporting rifle used a 10-shot rotary magazine that would have required extensive design changes if a different number of rounds had been required after 1994.

Even though the assault weapons ban expired in 2005, certain states and localities maintain the 10-shot magazine limit for guns either sold or owned in their jurisdictions. These laws have been challenged by the NRA, which claims "defensive" use of a gun might require a magazine with more than a 10-round capacity. Not only is there no data to prove that defensive gun use requires ammunition capacities in excess of 10 rounds, but legal arguments defending hi-cap magazines never mention *offensive* gun use.

12. What is an Assault Weapon?

If you take the issue of gun violence prevention seriously, sooner or later you will find yourself in discussion, debate, or an argument with someone who believes that any gun which is legally available for purchase and ownership in the United States is a sporting weapon, and should not be confused or mislabeled as an "assault" weapon because "assault" weapons are only full-auto guns that are issued to military troops on the field of battle.

The purpose of this little manual was to give you all the necessary information you need to understand the basic technical issues and nomenclature that appear in discussions about guns. But this manual has another goal as well. Because it is also written to help you think through the issue of lethality as it applies to all firearms and, in particular, to those types of guns, the most lethal types of guns, that are designed for one purpose and one purpose only, and that is to deliver lethal force against human beings, which is simply another way of thinking about something we call an "assault."

An assault is a physical attack. And it doesn't matter where or when this physical attack takes place, it is still an assault. Of course we can always pretend that some assaults are different from others because, after all, if you are defending rather than attacking, then obviously you are not trying to hurt someone else so much as you are trying to prevent yourself from getting hurt.

Which is all fine and well except for one little thing. Most people who defend themselves with a gun aren't being attacked by someone with a gun. On rare occasions perhaps it's true, but generally speaking, gun assaults usually grow out of an ongoing dispute or altercation between two individuals, and then one of them pulls out a gun. So it really doesn't matter whether you are the attacker or the defender. If you are holding the gun, then you are committing the assault.

But that's only true for certain types of guns, which was the point of this little book. Obviously, someone holding a double-barreled shotgun, a bolt-action rifle or a 22-caliber target revolver could assault someone else with that gun. But that's not what those guns were designed to do. They were designed to be used for hunting or sport, which is how they are almost always used.

But someone who buys a semi-automatic rifle that can deliver 60 rounds of high-powered ammunition in less than a minute isn't using that gun to shoot Big Bird out of a tree. And someone who buys a concealable pistol that can instantly reload multiple magazines containing 20 highly-lethal handgun rounds or more isn't going to use that gun to qualify for membership on a competitive shooting team.

So bear this in mind the next time you find yourself in conversation with an ardent supporter of gun "rights" who truly believes that every gun, no matter how lethal, is no different from every other type of gun. Guns are different, they are used differently, and their use produces different and sometimes tragic results.

I hope this little book helps you understand those differences and I look forward to your feedback at: mike@mikethegunguy.com.

READER SELF-TEST

Here are some questions that might get thrown at you by folks who don't believe (or understand) the lethality of guns. Answers follow the questions.

1. *Question:* The Supreme Court says I can own any kind of gun I want to own. Why should I let you decide which guns are too lethal for me to own?

    Answer: The Supreme Court said in 2008 that the 2nd Amendment gave Americans the "right" to keep a handgun in their home for self-defense. It did not define the type of handgun and it specifically gave government the right to regulate the commerce of firearms.

2. *Question:* Assault weapons are used by the military and fire full-automatic; modern sporting rifles fire semi-automatic. Why do you say that a modern sporting rifle is an assault weapon?

    Answer: The rifle currently used by the U.S. armed forces fires in both automatic and semi-automatic modes. Do soldiers use the semi-automatic mode because it is less lethal? No, they use it when the tactical situation requires it.

3. *Question:* If I can only carry 10 rounds in my pistol, the criminals will use hi-cap magazines and I will be outgunned. What do I do?

Answer: In the highly unlikely event that you actually would use a gun to defend yourself, there is no credible evidence that gunfights ever extend beyond 3-4 shots fired, except when they are used in mass shootings.

4. *Question:* How I choose to defend myself is a very personal decision. Why should I let government make that determination for me?

   Answer: You do not have a right to privacy if your behavior creates risks for others, such as using highly lethal guns.

5. *Question:* Why should hi-capacity magazines be banned when the government could not find that banning hi-cap magazines from 1995 through 2005 had any effect on gun violence rates?

   Answer: Because hi-capacity magazines increase lethality and lethal things should be regulated.

6. *Question:* By banning what you call "lethal" guns and feeding devices, aren't you just trying to get rid of all guns?

   Answer: No. I want my community to be safe.

7. *Question:* I am a law-abiding citizen who has never committed a violent act of any kind. Why should I be forced to use a magazine that only holds 10 rounds because some nut shot 100 people in an Orlando club?

Answer: The nut was also law-abiding until he decided to kill and wound more than 100 people with his legally purchased gun. We regulate lethal things because it's easier than trying to regulate people before they do something wrong.

8. *Question:* If an AR-15 rifle needs to be regulated because it's too lethal for civilian use, why not also regulate handguns that the military uses like Beretta or Glock?

   Answer: Because it's not just the magazine capacity that makes an AR-15 more lethal than other semi-automatic rifles, it's also the design of the gun.

9. *Question:* I like to hunt small and medium-sized game with my AR-15. What's wrong with that?

   Answer: Nothing. But you don't need a 30-round magazine to hunt deer.

10. *Question:* Why pick on guns? Twice as many people are attacked each year with knives than with guns.

    Answer: Which is why we regulate knives by banning possession of switchblades and automatic blades.